MOMTRAS

Mantras for Mindful Moms

Kristine McGlinchey-Yap

MOMTRAS

Cover design and layout:
Natalie Calzadilla: www.natalie1love.com

For information regarding special discounts for bulk purchases of this book, for charitable donation, or for speaking engagements, please visit www.ommommas.com.

ISBN: 9798654553966

Published by Kristine McGlinchey-Yap

Printed in the United States of America

A Blessing to the Divine Mother

May the reader be blessed with favor, love and compassion.

With honor and recognition from all the divine mothers who have come before her and will come after her.

May all our children be safe, loved and cared for with an open heart and a conscious mind.

The Journey Starts Here

When you become a mother you go through a shift - energetically, physically, mentally and spiritually.

Motherhood demands everything from you, your time, energy, attention, and presence.

It's truly one of the most powerful roles a woman can take on. It's beautiful, all-encompassing and it binds you to a soul that has chosen you, forever.

I'm a firm believer in "you are what you think" and as a first-time mother my thoughts were often from a place of self-defeat.

As I held my newborn baby girl in my arms I constantly wondered if I was a good mother, or if I was making the right decisions about how to take care of her every day.

I felt so much pressure to know everything and to be perfect. If I didn't know something, if I wasn't perfect - I was failing.

I learned to take it one day at a time.

MOMTRAS

While I don't have it all figured it out, what I do know for sure is that some days you won't know how you made it through, but you will.

You'll love so hard and so intensely that it will hurt.

You'll burn yourself out questioning if you're doing enough.

Just remember, don't forget to breathe.

Here and now - this is your moment.

This is your time to rejuvenate your mind, and to reflect on how far you've come in your journey.

My hope is that these Momtras act as simple reminders to the power and beauty you possess.

May they bring you a sense of hope, encouragement and wrap around you in comfort when you need it the most.

And above all, may they serve as a reminder that you are doing an amazing job.

How to Use Momtras

Mantras are words, sacred sounds, prayers or phrases used in meditation.

By continuously reciting them they are believed to create deep inner shifts.

The energy of the words raises its vibration having a positive effect on the mind and body.

Use your Momtras to achieve inner peace, realign with your spirit and purpose, and to connect to the higher power within you.

Go page by page and feel the inner truth each one holds for you or turn to a page randomly for instant clarity on how to approach a certain situation with ease.

Clear your mind.

Inhale and exhale.

Tune in to the energy of each Momtra and with an open heart and mind allow them to guide and support you.

I am more than good enough.

We are never as smart, attractive or well put together as all the other moms. If only we could be like them.

Except they are looking at us, wishing that they had what we have.

We view ourselves from a lens of "less-than." A vicious cycle of comparison that tells us we're not worthy, or we're not enough.

Every day you get out of bed and you do your best.

Some days it's harder to pull off than others, but here you are giving it your all.

The way you take care of your child is admirable. The love you give them, the attention, the praise, even on those messy days where things seem to crumble around you – yes, even on those days – you are more than good enough.

Motherhood isn't simple. It's a delicate balance of self-lessness and compassion.

The self-defeating words and thoughts end here.

Patience is a practice.

Take a deep breath in and a deep breath out.

You tell yourself you'll be more patient, but in the next breath you're yelling from across the room.

That's completely okay.

It takes practice to accept that we cannot be in control of everything.

Messes will be made, words will be used as weapons, actions will upset us.

We're still here. And these moments are just that. Moments in time that we can never get back.

While we're fighting to run out of the door on time, or to clean up toys from off of the floor, remember you will never get this moment back.

It's okay to be late or to get a little messy sometimes.

Life is meant to be playful, to be fun, to be savored and not rushed through.

Practice patience and everything will flow.

I radiate kindness.

Why is it that we treat strangers kinder than we treat ourselves and our families?

When we allow ourselves to receive and spread kindness, something wonderful happens.

Even in moments when you may not feel kind or giving, allow yourself to align with love.

Imagine a bright, white light radiating from your heart.

This light is shaped like a sphere and it is warm and comforting.

The sphere circles you, bringing you a feeling of joy and contentment.

This light is replenishing you with love and kindness.

Now that you feel complete, you are ready to share the light.

Extend your light by sending thoughts of love and kindness to your family, then to your friends, to your neighbors, to your city, to your state, to your country, to your continent and now to the world.

Your kindness is contagious.

I am present.

We are constantly worrying about what happens next - what should we have for dinner, what should we wear tomorrow, what do the kids need this week?

We live in a continuous state of anxiety, pressure and overwhelm thinking about the future. Meanwhile we miss what is right in front of us.

The time we spend on moments that haven't even happened yet, means the less time we have to enjoy the ones that we're in.

Have you ever stood still enough to enjoy the way your child looks up and smiles at you, or to stop and smell the scent of a freshly bathed baby?

Our children grow up in the blink of an eye and we reflect thinking if only we could have one more hug, one more snuggle, one more nap with them.

Enjoy these moments now, not as memories but as a special part of your day.

Stare a little longer. Hold a little tighter. Love a little harder.

I am not perfect, and
I am not expected to be.

Your ability to show up as yourself is true perfection.

Women, especially mothers, place unrealistic expectations on ourselves to have it all figured out, to know all of the things, to be it all and to do it all – effortlessly.

Our children do not need to see a perfect mom who has it all figured out.

They need to see a mom who figures it out as she goes, who isn't afraid to make mistakes and to admit when she's wrong.

One who cries and then laughs. One who forgives herself and others.

Let's teach our children to embrace challenges and obstacles so that they can move through them, not get deterred by them.

You have the strength to move mountains but that does not mean you have to carry those mountains with you.

Mistakes define us and are all a part of this beautiful journey.

I honor my child's individual journey

Parents only want the very best for their children and sometimes what we want for them isn't necessarily what is true to who they are.

We are not in control of our children's lives.

That is not our role. Our place is to guide and support them.

To lead them to become the best version of themselves that they can be.

The best version of *themselves*. Not who *we* think they are or want them to be.

When we try to control our children or project our unaccomplished dreams onto them, we are limiting them from pursuing their true purpose and keeping them from what nourishes their soul.

Our children will make choices that we don't support or agree with. That's a given.

But we get to keep an open mind and ongoing dialogue that allows them to express their opinions to feel seen and heard.

They are on their own journey we are here to keep them safe on their path.

I am supported.

You are a superhero. But even Wonder Woman had the Justice League.

Although we are fully capable, we don't have to do everything by ourselves.

Asking for help doesn't make you weak or a failure. It makes you strong and resilient.

We can't wear all the hats, do all the things and be expected to not feel overwhelmed or exhausted.

Whether it's a spouse, partner, friend, family member, or a hired helper, raising children requires a community.

People want to help us more than we think they do. Allowing others to step in gives them a sense of purpose.

Start by asking yourself these two questions:

What areas can I use support in?

How would I feel if I received support in these areas?

Next, ask for support and be open to receiving it.

I recognize and honor my strength.

It's amazing how strong you are.

You've endured heartache, cried tears of joy and have experienced grief.

There were times when it may have felt like all hope was lost, or you couldn't take just one second more.

But you pulled through.

Here you are, stronger than ever. More powerful than ever.

You did what they thought you couldn't, what you thought you couldn't.

And as you read these pages, you are filled with a renewed sense of power and validation.

Nothing can defeat you. You are a divine mother.

There is a circle of light and love that protects you.

Its warm glow keeps you going when you feel like you no longer can. You are a warrior.

I am in charge of
co-creating a life that I love.

You are more than a mother.

You are a dreamer.

When you wake up in the morning how do you want to feel?

Everything you've ever dreamed of and more is available to you, you just have to be open to receiving it.

Just as you birthed life, you are a co-creator of your own life.

You have the power to live a life that is full of happiness, abundance and success – however that may look for you.

Some days it may feel as if you're stuck or not going anywhere.

Just close your eyes and feel into that space of trust.

Honor and recognize that there is a plan for you that will unravel at the most beautiful time.

You have the power to live the life you choose.

Self-care is not selfish.

With a house full of children, a long list of to-dos and a never-ending pile of laundry/dishes/toys, there may never seem like enough time to take care of yourself.

We work until we're exhausted, we keep moving, going and doing.

We smile and power through it until the smile fades, the impatience wears in, our body aches and we can't stand the sight of ourselves in the mirror.

Prioritizing self-care is a necessity.

In order to be strong mentally, emotionally and spiritually for your family, you must put yourself on a pedestal.

Not every moment will be as indulgent as going to the spa, but even the slightest act such as an at-home facial, manicure or even taking the afternoon off to read a book, will do wonders.

Self-care means saving space to do something good for yourself.

When you feel your best, you are your best.

I approach stressful situations
with peace and clarity.

There will be moments when we allow our frustration to get the best of us.

As the anger starts to well up, take a moment to view the situation as an outside participant.

Breathe. Reset.

You are full of love and light.

Whatever this situation looks like for you, it's only momentary and will pass.

Nothing is worth losing your peace over.

You are equipped to handle any problem or issue that comes your way.

You were made for this.

The situation is clear to you and you can resolve any issues with ease.

A sense of calm overcomes you as you relax into knowing.

You are grounded, releasing negative energy and replacing it with a renewed sense of peace.

Love flows to and through me.

As mothers, we have so much love to give.

Our hearts long to care and nurture our children, but we must also remember to give ourselves the same amount of adoration and love in return.

You above all, are worthy of your own love.

You deserve to be loved and cared for in the way that makes you feel valued too.

At times you may feel depleted, as if you've given all of yourself and have nothing left to give.

We possess unlimited amounts of love and goodness within us.

Our supplies will never run out.

You are a beacon of comfort and joy to yourself and others.

A beautiful white light of loving energy emanates from your heart and envelops those around you.

All that is requested of you is that you lead with love.

Forgiveness is healing.

We all make mistakes.

Sometimes intentional, other times neglectful, but often accidental.

How we move forward from those mistakes is what matters most.

Do not allow the mistakes of others to keep you from your happiness, purpose or peace.

When we forgive others we give ourselves permission to heal.

We release the burden of negativity, unease and mistrust and we open up to love, clarity and hope.

Forgiveness doesn't mean allowing people to take advantage of you.

It means not holding on to feelings that are holding you back.

When we forgive others – and ourselves - we are liberated from the heaviness of having to carry around that emotional baggage.

When you are ready just say, "I forgive you and I release you."

My feelings are valid.

We want nothing more than to be the perfect mom who says, thinks and does all the perfect things.

It's okay to have days where you don't want to be it all or do it all.

It's perfectly normal to fantasize about being alone on a deserted island for a day.

You're allowed to be sad, overjoyed, angry, happy, resentful, motivated and everything in between.

Your feelings matter. They are valid and they should come first.

Question why it is you're feeling the way you are, take a closer look at how you're processing and handling everything around you.

Mothers make time for everyone else's feelings, make sure to sit with yours.

You're allowed to talk about how you feel and most importantly without judgment.

Having feelings doesn't make you less of a mother. It makes you human.

Every day is a celebration of the
beautiful woman I am.

You deserve to be celebrated.

Look at how far you've come and all that you've accomplished.

Celebrate your breath, the oxygen pumping to your heart, the start or completion of another day.

Everything you do holds power and energy. Make sure both are directed toward positivity.

When we give ourselves praise we honor our journey and acknowledge how much we are truly capable of.

There is so much to celebrate about being a mother.

That face that lights up your life, your body that is a temple of creation, your ability to love beyond measure and the endless reserves of strength and wisdom you possess.

Every day is a new chance to celebrate the amazing miracle that life is.

Celebrate how beautiful your life is.

I begin and end each day
in gratitude.

To be grateful is to be in awe of all life offers us.

Gratitude is being mindful and feeling a deep sense of appreciation for all that surrounds you.

You can be grateful for the wind, the birds, this book.

Centering and focusing on gratitude allows us to gain perspective on the blessings in our lives, especially on days when we need it the most.

Having a daily gratitude practice reframes our thoughts and allows us to shift to a more positive mindframe.

At the beginning and end of each day list everything you are grateful for.

If it helps, you can write it down and keep a journal.

I am grateful for this time to myself.

I am grateful for moments of peace.

I am grateful for quiet reflection.

There are so many things to be grateful for, nothing is too big or small.

My life holds infinite possibilities.

We are not naturally bound by limits.

We are the ones who place limits on ourselves, our children, and our families.

Is it a new career, home, vacation, or hobby that you fantasize about?

What would it feel like for you to be living your dreams?

What would it look like having everything you imagined?

Whatever it is that gives you purpose – the kind of purpose that makes your heart happy – go after it.

We often get tangled in the web of "how."

How am I going to accomplish this, how can I get there, how will I find the money?

How traps us into believing we're not good enough.

Let's replace how with now.

There are no limits to what you can do, who you can be – you are infinite.

I live a life of purpose.

There are times in our lives where we may feel lost, especially as we transition into motherhood.

We search for signs, whispers and messages in hopes that they will tell us what to do or who we should be.

We're constantly changing, growing and evolving as individuals.

Your purpose today may not be the same as it is tomorrow.

As a mother, you are a guiding light and a symbol of love and comfort.

As a woman, that's up to you to find out.

What excites you just thinking of the possibility of it?

Some are here to guide and serve others, some are here to lead, some are here to make the world a better place by simply just existing.

Whichever category you fall into, trust that you walk with confidence and clarity on your purpose.

I am mindful.

Being mindful is being an observer to your thoughts and actions. It's allowing yourself to feel and experience every moment.

When we allow each moment to unfold in the beautiful way that it is meant to rather than trying to control it, we can appreciate it so much more. This includes words and actions.

When we consider how what we say and do makes others feel, we are aware more than ever the energy and impact simple things hold.

Taking a moment to clear your mind and meditate is a mindful practice that regenerates and centers you.

Investing in your mental and spiritual strength creates a ripple effect as these areas touch all facets of your life.

Mindful reminders:

Lead with love.

Communicate with compassion.

Guide with gratitude.

Judgment does not serve me.

It's much easier to pass judgment on to people and situations, than it is to take the time to understand them.

Our minds create stories about everything before we see, hear or experience what's actually happening.

With our children we tend to see everything through a critical lens. Criticizing their every action, gesture or opinion.

We even judge ourselves for judging.

We may also base our experiences on things that have happened in the past which is not a fair comparison because the present moment is the only one that matters.

When you feel yourself starting to judge a person, situation or event, choose a different perspective.

Judgment creates separation. When we learn to disconnect from it, we create unity and harmony in our lives.

Release judgment and choose compassion instead.

Listening is just as
important as speaking.

Have you ever just wanted someone to listen to you without giving their opinion or advice?

I imagine that's how our children must feel when we want to solve their problems and have all the answers.

To truly understand how someone feels you must listen.

When we give someone our undivided attention and allow them to communicate their feelings without judgment or shame, we allow them to release their worries and begin the healing process.

People want to be heard, they want to be seen and treated as though what they have to say matters.

When you listen, you provide comfort and a silent guidance by being attentive and present.

By listening to your child, you are validating their feelings.

Letting them know that they are honored and respected.

My intuition is my compass.

You can read, research and Google everything you think you need to know or do, but when it comes down to it, you already know.

Everything you need to know is already found within you.

Our intuition acts as an internal compass that alerts us when something feels right or wrong.

Learn to engage and trust that natural inclination.

Listening and trusting ourselves is important as mothers because we receive so much divine wisdom when it comes down to how to care for our families.

When we parent from a place of trust and knowing, we can make more sound decisions.

Don't spend all of your time doubting or questioning yourself.

Be open to receiving all the knowledge you possess within.

I am committed to showing up
as my best self each day.

When we are out of alignment with our mind, body and spirit, we don't have the capacity to approach people or situations from a place of clarity.

By establishing a morning routine that includes practicing gratitude and giving yourself a few minutes to send love and compassion to yourself, you are preparing for an amazing day ahead.

Even if things don't unfold as peacefully as the day started you can always connect with the intention to be your best self.

Give yourself grace and feel through each emotion as it comes up.

It's not about pushing your feelings to the side and replacing them with a false sense of positivity.

It's about honoring what comes up for you, recognizing it and releasing it.

Being your best means being committed to vulnerability, authenticity and compassion.

I release all feelings of guilt.

Guilt stems from our feelings of worthiness.

As mothers this may manifest when we feel like we let someone down, we didn't do enough, we aren't attentive enough, or we made a mistake.

It's almost as if the feelings of guilt have become a natural by-product of being a mother.

We are allowed to be more than a mother.

We are allowed to want/need/ask for more.

You don't need permission to be the fullest expression of who you are. A child doesn't change that.

We are all expansive, limitless beings who have a role and purpose to fill.

Don't miss out on yours by being tied down to feelings of guilt that leave you wading through mud.

You'd be guilty to not live the life you were made to.

Eeverything is in alignment with my
highest and greatest good.

We go through tough times in our lives.

Situations we feel like we can't endure, moments when we look up to the sky and ask, "Why me?"

It's all a part of the grand design of our lives that we aren't capable of fully appreciating until the grief, the anxiety, and the worry subsides.

There is beauty on the other side of the chaos, or the mess we sometimes find ourselves in.

If we trust, if we have faith, if we keep pushing through it, we will emerge stronger, more capable and wiser than we were before.

Scars are marks that remind us that we can handle anything that comes our way.

You are resilient.

Nothing can dim your light or bring you down.

You were made to overcome obstacles and hardships with ease.

Everything's coming together for your greatest good.

I choose me.

Time, attention, love, understanding – all things that we naturally and unconditionally provide to everyone around us.

The problem is that we give it all away, forgetting to offer them to the most important person – you!

We are not taught to put ourselves on a pedestal.

Society tells us that we have to put everyone else before us to be good mothers.

When we love, care and honor ourselves we allow our hearts to expand and hold space for everyone around us.

Without first providing ourselves with the necessary attention, we can't be fully present or functional for those who need us.

Throughout the day remind yourself, "I choose me."

Choose to be kind, to send yourself love and care.

When in doubt you are the best choice you can make.

I define my worth.

Don't let anyone try to tell you what you're worth.

You set the standard.

Some will try to make you feel worth-less, by telling you how to be a good mother/wife/partner/business woman.

How you choose to show up in these categories is worth more than anything they can "teach" you.

Don't they know that you're all-knowing, and powerful in your own right?

Your worth is not measured by anyone else's criteria or judgment.

When we stand up for what we believe in and are held accountable for our decisions, we define our worth by standing firm in our beliefs.

When we voice our opinions and remain confident, we establish our worth.

You are worth more than anyone could ever put into value.

54

I am abundant.

How many times a day do you catch yourself thinking from a place of lack or scarcity?

"I don't have the time to do that."

"I'll never make that much money."

We're conditioned to think that we can't attain the things that we want whether material or emotional.

Again, we find ourselves operating from a place of worth-less-ness rather than worthiness.

Infinite resources and possibilities exist for all of us. We just have to tune in to the energy and receive it.

Imagine a bright white light flowing to and through you.

This light represents abundance and you are operating on the same frequency that it is.

You are in harmony with abundance.

Prosperity, good fortune, happiness, good health – you are abundant in every area of your life.

I am a blessing to others.

It's easy to forget that we have the ability to heal, nurture and support others in such a powerful way.

Being a mother is a beautiful blessing.

We hold within us the light and love of creation itself.

We are the caretakers of our communities, and even bigger picture the world itself.

When we raise mindful, kind and compassionate children we are birthing a more mindful, kind and compassionate world.

It's important that we hold on to this positive energy, rather than allowing ourselves to get caught up in the stresses of everyday life.

When we allow ourselves to feel, receive and be open to the blessings that surround us, we can share that with everyone around us.

Close your eyes and receive any blessings you may have been blocking from entering your life.

Your life is a blessing, you are a blessing.

Happiness is a choice.

Most people think that happiness is a goal or destination.

When our children do this, when we buy that thing, or when we become this person that's when we'll be happy.

Happiness is a choice we get to make every single minute, hour and second.

It's not as elusive as we make it out to be. It's that simple and easy. We tend to make life more complicated than it is.

A shift in mindset is all that it takes.

Feeling overwhelmed?

Choose happiness instead.

Feeling angry?

Choose happiness instead.

Fear/worry/frustration – I'd rather be happy.

Each moment you spend not being happy, is a moment that you can't get back.

Choose happiness.

I am in complete alignment with my mind, body and spirit.

When we are aligned with the energy of our minds, bodies and spirit we live with clarity and purpose.

Distractions, stressors, and overwhelming emotions often jar us out of alignment.

Repeat this Momtra often throughout the day to recenter yourself and reset your internal balance and harmony.

When you live in alignment everything flows.

Nothing seems too out of reach or difficult.

Your mind, body and spirit are operating in complete harmony. They are working for your highest and greatest good.

Ground yourself in knowing that you are fully supported and committed to your purpose, intention and this moment.

A white light flows through your body seamlessly, filtering out and releasing everything that does not serve you.

You are completely aligned.

I establish clear boundaries.

Women have a high threshold when it comes to entertaining ideas, people, and even situations that we know we shouldn't be.

We're natural people pleasers.

We're conditioned to feel like we have to please everyone (except ourselves) in order to be valued, respected and worthy.

It's time to establish clear boundaries.

Whether it's with a spouse, parents, family, in-laws, friends or your children – you get to decide what and who you do things for and when.

There is no room left in your journey to feel like you're being taken for granted, advantage of, or disregarded.

When you establish clear boundaries, you set a standard for yourself and those around you.

Boundaries are necessary for self-care, mental health and growth.

I attract meaningful connections.

The transition into motherhood can sometimes feel like a lonely journey.

It's a time of deep transformation, healing and growth. The creation of a bond, unlike any other – between mother and child.

We may find it difficult to relate to others who are close to us in the ways that we are used to.

When the visitors stop coming by, when people stop asking how you're doing and silence and the sound of your baby crying is all that's left, you don't want to feel alone.

We seek counsel and comfort in other mothers who understand the ups-and-downs and the highs-and-lows of raising a child.

Close your eyes and imagine feeling surrounded by warm, positive energies, there to uplift and comfort you.

You are attracting meaningful connections who will support you and be here for you when you need it most.

I am present in each moment.

When we honor each moment with our presence, we are able to fully enjoy our lives and the company of those around us.

Too many things aim to distract us and keep us disconnected - cell phones, social media, television, tablets, video games - the list goes on and on!

When we're doing too many things at once we miss out on the things that truly matter most.

The way your baby looks up and smiles at you, or a butterfly gently resting on a flower.

Moments like these come and go so fast, but when we are present we can appreciate the way they make us feel.

That feeling will stay with us forever.

Much more meaningful than scrolling through a feed or timeline.

Don't miss out on the ordinary moments that make life extraordinary.

My body is beautiful.

Do you ever take a moment to acknowledge how amazing your body is?

Our arms are blankets for our newborns.

Our breasts are soft pillows and sources of nutrition for our infants.

Our laps are the perfect resting place for a loved one.

Stretch marks are the reminder that our bodies are just as expansive as our possibilities.

Your body is a beautiful temple.

It holds the magic of creation and wonder of life itself.

Look in the mirror and admire everything about your body.

The folds, the curves, the color – it is all perfect.

Wrap your arms around yourself and breathe love into your body.

You are beautiful.

I welcome and embrace change.

Our lives change in an instant.

From having a newborn to a teenager in the blink of an eye.

It can be hard to accept that our children grow up so fast.

The minute they learn to walk they walk farther away from us, and then they learn to drive and they drive away from us.

Watching a child gain independence and become their own person is a remarkable blessing.

Welcome each stage, and each milestone with optimism.

There is so much joy in knowing that you've supported and guided your child to where they are today.

Embrace the journey and recognize that growth and progress is all part of the process.

Don't forget to celebrate yourself because you made it here too!

I take nothing for granted.

Each day is a gift.

Each breath is another chance.

Each moment is a reminder of possibility.

It's easy to take what we have in our lives for granted. Easier to take who we have in our lives for granted.

Don't let one day go by without telling the people that you love how much you appreciate them and how grateful you are to know them.

Life is a precious thing.

Let's not get caught up in the tedious aspects of life - the messiness, the tears, the fights, the worrying.

There is so much more to be thankful for.

Somewhere out there right now, someone is praying for what you have.

Let's not lose sight of what truly matters.

Close your eyes and express gratitude to all that you are thankful for in your life.

Trust the journey.

We want so badly to be in control of every outcome.

How our day unfolds, who our children grow up to be, what and when we accomplish something.

We want life to operate on our personal timetable.

We're so busy planning for the future that we miss out on the magic of the day-to-day experience.

The more we try to control people and outcomes the more out of control our lives become.

That's when we find ourselves spiraling in feelings of disappointment and overwhelm.

Allow your life to flow with limitless possibilities.

Trust that your life is unfolding exactly as it should, in the right time.

With faith, everything you are hoping for is coming to pass.

I reciprocate respect.

Our children are born into this world adoring and looking up to us.

When they learn how to interact with their environment, test boundaries and think for themselves it may feel like respect is a revolving door.

Respect is gained, earned and reciprocated.

If we want our children to respect us, we have to show them that we respect them and everyone we interact with.

We have to lead by example.

When we treat others with respect, kindness and admiration our children will pick up on the same behaviors.

Even when we think they're not watching us, children have keen intuition.

They sense our energy and pick up on little gestures.

Respect others and be respected in return.

Laughter is medicine for the soul.

Responsibility and duty often take the primary focus of our roles as mothers.

In your household are dad or the grandparents always the fun ones?

Laughter gives us a boost of energy; it clears away the debris of stress and anxiety.

Laughing reminds us that life is good, that it isn't always about to-do lists, cleaning or running around doing errands.

Remember that little girl inside of you.

The one who loved to play and run around all day with no agenda.

Remember how liberating that felt.

Let your hair down, make a silly face, play a game and let the kids make a mess.

Tell a joke, laugh at nothing.

Be in the moment and connect with joy.

Whatever the ailment, laughter is the best course of treatment.

I value my health and wellbeing.

As a mother your health and wellbeing is a priority.

You research for hours on end the best foods, creams, clothes and treatments for your children.

Treat yourself the same way.

Take a look at the products you're using, the foods you're eating and how you can incorporate simple fitness routines in your day.

It's time to nourish your mind, body and spirit.

While meal planning for the kids make sure your nutritional goals are met too.

It can be hard when you're constantly on the go but take the time to listen and give your body what it needs.

Sometimes you just need to slow down and take it easy.

Make your wellbeing a priority.

A healthy mother is a powerful mother.

Through consciousness
I find healing.

A conscious parent is not a perfect one.

It is one who is aware that they are not perfect, and they consciously try to resolve any issues they experience in that area.

Parenting exposes traumas from our pasts.

Wounds from childhood that we've kept hidden.

As a defense mechanism, we don't self-reflect and heal, we move on and bury our traumas. Through introspection you will find healing.

When you work through triggers and observe them from a distance, you can release all of that heavy energy that doesn't belong to you anymore.

In consciousness you find true liberation.

Freedom from the limiting beliefs and behavioral patterns that have been holding you back.

This newfound freedom allows you to better woman and better mother.

I am empowered.

Do you remember the last time someone made you feel like you didn't matter?

Was it in the last week, month or year?

My hope is that you never feel that way again.

You are stronger than anyone gives you credit for.

You are more beautiful than any words can describe.

You are a creator.

How can someone make you feel worth-less, than the priceless being you truly are?

Feel the power you possess.

Tap into that space where everything and anything is possible because you make it that way.

Your words matter.

Your feelings matter.

You matter.

Generational trauma ends with me.

We grow up with the trauma of our ancestors, the collective trauma of society and the ones we face ourselves.

We become adults who spread our unresolved hurt onto others, pass them down to our children and the vicious cycle continues.

It's scientifically proven that this becomes a part of our DNA and our biological make-up.

But it doesn't have to continue, it can end with you.

Your lineage deserves a new narrative.

You can honor your ancestors without having to carry the baggage of the past with you.

Through self-awareness and forgiveness, you can be set free.

Start a new chapter for your children and their children by setting intentions and blessings.

Release the past and thank it for its lessons.

My mind is open,
my heart is open.

As you release judgment, save space for new ideas and new ways of being.

Keep your mind open to the way your children choose to express themselves.

We live in a culture that is constantly evolving, shifting and cultivating new norms.

Don't be too eager to dismiss them.

When you have an open mind, your heart is open to accepting and sending love.

The heart and mind work in tandem to embrace and welcome new perspectives.

People will feel drawn to you and more receptive to sharing things with you knowing that they have a safe space to do so.

When you are feeling overly judgmental or critical, imagine a bright white light flowing from your heart to your mind.

Back and forth the light is transmitting comfort and warmth to your heart and mind to clear away any doubt or judgment.

I accept myself fully.

Have you grown tired of people and/or society constantly trying to tell you who to be, how to dress, what to think, how to parent, and on and on.

You are a work in progress - we all are.

You are allowed to change, to become a new person, to try new things, if and when you want to.

There is nothing you lack.

There is nothing you can do better, do more of or do less of, unless you decide it.

Where you are right now in life is perfect.

You are evolving, constantly learning and in the process of simultaneously becoming and unbecoming.

Accept that you are everything you need to be right now.

When you are ready for more you will pursue it.

Embrace who you are and who you are becoming.

I am successful.

Society is obsessed with failure.

So much so that we've conditioned ourselves to automatically choose failure as a default condition.

Did you try something new with the baby but they didn't like it?

You're not a failure you're an innovator.

Did you go after a new position at work but they gave it to someone else?

You're not a failure, you're brave for putting yourself out there and now you know you are ready to move on to bigger things.

Let's train our minds to choose success.

True failure is found in not trying.

If you tried, no matter the outcome, you're successful.

The energy of success is actually rooted in trying, but we get too attached to the outcome or result of our actions.

You are successful at everything you do.

94

I am my best when I get rest.

You don't win awards by depriving yourself of sleep, peace or stillness.

We are programmed to associate productivity with fatigue.

This "I have to stay busy" mindset doesn't serve us or our family if it's followed by burn-out.

You are allowed to nap, to take five minutes to meditate, to lay on the couch and watch reruns of whatever show makes you happy.

The house doesn't have to be spotless.

The laundry can pile up for a day.

You can order takeout.

This doesn't make you a "lazy mom."

This makes you a beautiful human who is honoring her limits, boundaries and needs.

You deserve a break.

You deserve a day, week or month off.

You are your best when you feel your best - so go and get some rest!

Mindset is more than Momtras.

97

While it is certainly helpful and a powerful practice to recite these Momtras, your mindset needs more of a commitment from you in order to shift.

Feel the words and how they land in your body. Embrace the energy you feel when reciting each Momtra.

Actively commit to healing.

Do the work that you know is required of you to create change.

What comes up for you?

In what ways are you being called to heal?

What areas do you need support in?

Get to know yourself. Notice what things irritate you, what makes you happy, what you love doing and not doing.

And be ok with what comes up.

Recognize and honor yourself from a place of compassion and love.

That's the power of a sound mind.

Motherhood takes a community.

Somewhere in time and space, we lost the sacred ways in which motherhood was regarded.

Centuries ago, mothers were revered and highly respected.

We were praised, catered to and treated lavishly by our communities.

Let's go back to the old ways.

Let's revisit how we can make motherhood a sacred tradition again.

Let's uplift one another.

Let's offer to help one another.

Struggling mom, I see you trying to hold it together and to you I extend my hand.

Take it and we will do this together.

We are one.

Our children are born out of heavenly creation.

Let's create community and end separation.

OM MOMMAS

OM Mommas is a community for mindful mothers interested in reclaiming their power and raising their children through conscious parenting techniques that encourage healing, self-development and awareness.

No matter what stage of motherhood you're in, OM Mommas provides support, guidance and advocacy with products and services that align with your mind, body and spirit.

As a special gift for purchasing the book, access exclusive resources in a private, members only community. To join, visit www.ommommas.com/momtras.

Connect on Facebook and Instagram: @OMMommas

Has this book inspired you to create your own Momtras? List yours here:

____

____

____

____

____

____

____

____

____

____

I want to hear from you!

Share your personal Momtras with me by emailing **kristine@ommommas.com**.

MOMTRAS

The perfect accompaniment throughout a woman's motherhood journey.

Written by a first-time mother who found comfort and inspiration in reciting daily mantras, *Momtras*, is a companion to mindful mothers who need a reminder of the strength and infinite wisdom they possess.

Kristine McGlinchey-Yap is the mindful momma behind OM Mommas, a community dedicated to conscious parenting. With over a decade of experience in corporate communications, she has transitioned her leadership skills into providing women with guidance into stepping into their journey to motherhood. With loyal advocacy she supports and encourages women to claim their power and own their motherhood experience by making choices that align with their mind, body and spirit. She believes women have the potential to birth a more loving world when they become more caring, empowered and conscious themselves. For resources and more information, please visit www.ommommas.com. Join the community on Facebook and Instagram at @OMMommas.